TO

FROM

DATE

KEN PETERSEN

Farm Sweet Farm

A BUSHEL OF REASONS TO LOVE COUNTRY LIVING

Tyndale House Publishers
Carol Stream, Illinois

LIVING EXPRESSIONS

COLLECTION

Living Expressions invites you to explore God's Word in a way that is refreshing to your spirit and restorative to your soul.

Visit Tyndale online at tyndale.com.

Tyndale, Tyndale's quill logo, *Living Expressions*, and the Living Expressions logo are registered trademarks of Tyndale House Ministries.

Farm Sweet Farm: A Bushel of Reasons to Love Country Living

Designed by Lindsey Bergsma

For information about special discounts for bulk purchases, please contact Tyndale House Publishers at csresponse@tyndale.com, or call 1-855-277-9400.

ISBN 978-1-4964-5395-2

Printed in China

28	27	26	25	24	23	22
7	6	5	4	3	2	1

Contents

When the ground soaks up the
falling rain and bears a good crop for
the farmer, it has God's blessing.

HEBREWS 6:7, NLT

Plant your seed in the morning
and keep busy all afternoon, for you
don't know if profit will come from one
activity or another—or maybe both.

ECCLESIASTES 11:6, NLT

The country
life is to be
preferred; for
there we see the
works of God.

WILLIAM PENN,
*THE SELECT WORKS OF
WILLIAM PENN*

God's "Good Morning"

The good thing about waking up before dawn to do farm chores is that you get to see the country sunrise—God's unveiling of a painting he worked on all night. Fields of corn and wheat, stretching as far as you can see, emerge from the darkness, dappled in the early sun's pinks, purples, and golds. God doesn't need to send you a picture postcard from the corner store to remind you of who he is. On this country day, he will be present with you in the garden, with the animals, or in the barn—and in this quiet moment, he is saying to you, "Good morning!"

Let the fields and their crops burst
out with joy! Let the trees of the forest sing
for joy before the LORD, for he is coming!

PSALM 96:12-13, NLT

The Music of God

Sometimes a country morning is too beautiful for words. The dawning sun spreads along the horizon. A slight breeze rustles the wheat fields beyond the barn. Birds chirp, cows moo, and chickens cackle. A rooster crows, prompting the dog to reply, barking his happy "Good morning!" This is the music of God. He makes music everywhere, but here—where the fields extend as far as you can see to meet the sky—God's symphony seems most pure. Yes, listen, but also sing along. Maybe you could belt out a fun country song you love, or perhaps a hymn that you cherish. Whatever the song, your voice joining the orchestra of a country dawn is nothing less than worship. Tell God how much his music means to you this morning. Sing your praises to him for his merciful goodness.

Great is his faithfulness;
his mercies begin afresh each morning.

LAMENTATIONS 3:23, NLT

True
country music
is honesty,
sincerity, and
real life to
the hilt.

ATTRIBUTED TO
GARTH BROOKS

Every Dawn Is Different

The classic musical *Fiddler on the Roof* is about a Jewish family living in rural imperial Russia at the turn of the twentieth century. One of its most popular songs is "Sunrise, Sunset," in which the main character, Tevye, and his wife, Golde, wistfully reflect on where time went while they were busy raising a family. The lyrics and melody echo the rising and setting of the sun day after day. Maybe it can be a reminder for you to reflect as well on the course of time. If you feel as if life has passed you by, take comfort in knowing that each day's sunrise symbolizes God's faithfulness and reflects his glorious creativity. Every dawn is different, and every day has new possibilities.

Because of God's tender mercy, the morning light
from heaven is about to break upon us, to give light
to those who sit in darkness and in the shadow of
death, and to guide us to the path of peace.

LUKE 1:78-79, NLT

Heaven's Dew

Did you know the climate in many parts of the world is so dry that the only water available for sustaining crops is the early-morning dew? This glistening moisture at daybreak is truly God's provision. In the Bible, dew is also a symbol of unity and resurrection life (Psalm 133:3; Isaiah 26:19). Its blessing applies to us personally, to our lives and struggles. Are you trapped in a season of dryness, of parched life? Do you thirst for something new? Consider turning to the fountain of wisdom the Bible provides. Moses said, "Let my teaching fall on you like rain; let my speech settle like dew" (Deuteronomy 32:2, NLT). Immerse yourself in God's words, spoken through his prophets in the Bible. Let him water your life with heaven's dew.

May God give you of the dew of heaven,
of the fatness of the earth,
and plenty of grain and wine.
GENESIS 27:28

Blessed by GOD be his land: the best fresh dew from high heaven.

DEUTERONOMY 33:13, MSG

Heaven on Earth

Imagine you're spending some early-morning time in a beautiful garden, the air damp from the night. Dewdrops are puddled on flower petals, a breeze awakening their nectar and fragrance. It's almost as if heaven has come down to earth. Not surprising, for in the Bible, the Garden of Eden was mankind's original home; Jesus prayed in the garden of Gethsemane before his crucifixion; and the garden tomb was the site of his glorious resurrection. One of Christendom's most beloved hymns echoes Mary Magdalene's experience at the garden tomb: "I come to the garden alone, while the dew is still on the roses." The chorus proclaims, "And he walks with me, and he talks with me, and he tells me I am his own." Where is your personal garden—that setting of quiet, spiritual reflection? Be sure to go there soon to walk and talk with the Lord of your life.

She turned around and saw Jesus standing there, but she did not realize that it was Jesus. He asked her, "Woman, why are you crying? Who is it you are looking for?" Thinking he was the gardener, she said, "Sir, if you have carried him away, tell me where you have put him, and I will get him." Jesus said to her, "Mary."

JOHN 20:14-16, NIV

The one thing
that is worse
than a quitter is
the man who is
afraid to begin.

AMISH PROVERB

He Who Hesitates . . .

As you look ahead to your day, are you thinking about a chore or conversation you're dreading—something you've postponed over and over? What do you suppose might be the real reason for procrastinating? For some it's perfectionism—they want to do a task exactly right and don't want to get it wrong. For others it's the worry that people will respond negatively. Either way, fear is limiting. Know that God doesn't want you to be paralyzed. He wants you to "take up your bed and walk" (John 5:8)—so get going. You, as a child of God, are filled with his Spirit, and that gives you strength and courage. Through God's power, you can do this thing.

God has not given us a spirit of fear and timidity,
but of power, love, and self-discipline.

2 TIMOTHY 1:7, NLT

Listening to God

Perhaps you're a city dweller who has a fascination with the country. There is a case to be made for city life, too, although country-folk would have a hard time believing it. One problem with the urban landscape is that it's loud. Even at night, the noise of the city—cars honking, people yelling, music blasting—is exhausting, distracting. You can hardly hear yourself think. Our lives sometimes become a babble of sound and noise, just like a New York City street in July. During these times we may find it hard to discern God's voice. It might be that you need to take your prayer life to the country—even if in a virtual sense. Perhaps you need to find your own version of a farmhouse porch in the early evening. Sit down with God in the quiet, and listen to him talk to you. Let him feed you fresh clarity and direction as he cuts through the clatter of your life.

My sheep hear My voice,
and I know them, and they follow Me.

JOHN 10:27

Listen to me, and you will eat what is good.
You will enjoy the finest food. Come to me with your
ears wide open. Listen, and you will find life.

ISAIAH 55:2-3, NLT

Nor rural sights alone, but rural sounds exhilarate the spirit, and restore the tone of languid Nature.

WILLIAM COWPER, "THE TASK"

The Rhythm of Routine

In working the land, there's a regular schedule for preparing the soil, planting the seeds, watering the crops, and gleaning the harvest. It's a constant beat, a routine of life—a rhythm of seasons, months, and days. There's beauty in the routine, the rolling ebb and flow of the pattern. Whether you're farming, cooking, or teaching, or perhaps laboring at the office, in a shop, or at home, here's an idea: Find the rhythm of your work. Listen for the beat of divine music that God has composed. Remember: You are doing God's good will, so sing the song that he is singing.

For everything there is a season, a time for
every activity under heaven. A time to be born and
a time to die. A time to plant and a time to harvest. . . .
God has made everything beautiful for its own time.

ECCLESIASTES 3:1-2, 11, NLT

The LORD your God in your midst, the Mighty One,
will save; He will rejoice over you with gladness, He will quiet
you with His love, He will rejoice over you with singing.

ZEPHANIAH 3:17

*Earth laughs
in flowers.*

RALPH WALDO EMERSON,
"HAMATREYA"

The Joy of Spring

Those who live close to the earth see the hand of God in every season. But spring is especially welcome, when the first shoots of green break through the soil after a hard winter. God nudges life into the world again, as if he were chuckling, pleased once again with the world he so loves. Perhaps you have lived through a cold, dark winter. Maybe it's time to step outside into country spring-time. Listen for your heavenly Father's laughter as you blossom again into fresh patterns and colors.

You have turned for me my mourning
into dancing; you have put off my
sackcloth and clothed me with gladness.

PSALM 30:11

He will send showers of rain
so every field becomes a lush pasture.

ZECHARIAH 10:1, NLT

Blossoming Seeds

Johnny Appleseed is more famous, but Dr. David Fairchild may have done more than Johnny to seed America with new plants, fruits, and vegetables. In the early 1900s, Fairchild introduced the United States to new kinds of produce in the form of avocados, mangoes, and other exotic agricultural delights. It was also Fairchild who introduced cherry trees to Washington, DC. Eventually thousands were planted throughout the city, and even today their fragrant, beautiful blossoms are enjoyed every spring. What's growing in your garden these days? What seeds are you planting for others? With proper care and nurturing, they will blossom and bring springtime to the ones you love.

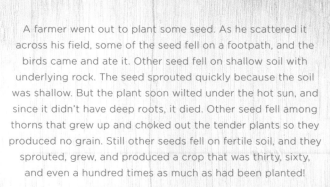

A farmer went out to plant some seed. As he scattered it across his field, some of the seed fell on a footpath, and the birds came and ate it. Other seed fell on shallow soil with underlying rock. The seed sprouted quickly because the soil was shallow. But the plant soon wilted under the hot sun, and since it didn't have deep roots, it died. Other seed fell among thorns that grew up and choked out the tender plants so they produced no grain. Still other seeds fell on fertile soil, and they sprouted, grew, and produced a crop that was thirty, sixty, and even a hundred times as much as had been planted!

MARK 4:3-8, NLT

A seed hidden
in the heart
of an apple
is an orchard
invisible.

KAHLIL GIBRAN,
JESUS THE SON OF MAN

Growing Great Fruit

As orchard farmers will tell you, despite the proverb, apple seeds don't grow good apple trees. The preferred method is *grafting*—the technique of taking parts of two apple trees and joining them to grow together. Yet the wisdom of the proverb still holds: You have great potential to produce great things—but not if you go it alone. This is the wisdom of the Bible as well: "As the branch cannot bear fruit of itself, unless it abides in the vine, neither can you, unless you abide in [Jesus]" (John 15:4). The "orchard invisible" is another name for your potential, and it can only come about if you have a thriving relationship with God. It's time to produce delicious fruit in life. Make sure you are grafted into him!

I am the vine, you are the branches.
He who abides in Me, and I in him, bears much
fruit; for without Me you can do nothing.

JOHN 15:5

Hands in the Soil

The new thing in agricultural technology may very well be—that's right—robots: machines that can till and plant and thresh without a human being driving them. Many farmers are not one bit happy about this, and rightfully so. It puts them on the sidelines and removes them from the soil. For many of us push-button, app-driven, Alexa-automated folks, though, we are more than happy to do life this way. How often in your connections with people do you opt to push a button from afar? As we experience life from the sidelines, we wonder why we're unfulfilled. There is much to be gained by actually tilling the soil of our relationships, getting our hands dirty in the loam of people and their needs. God wants you to be involved in this real work of life, for it is where you will find your true purpose and pleasure.

Those who work their land will
have abundant food, but those who chase
fantasies will have their fill of poverty.

PROVERBS 28:19, NIV

It all just seemed so good the way we had it

Back before everything became automatic

MIRANDA LAMBERT, "AUTOMATIC"

Lost and Found

The beauty of endless fields of wheat is a simple pleasure of life on many a farm. Their golden hue and wavy texture incite wonder. But those same enthralling vistas might sometimes present a darker experience for children. In one pioneer account, two toddlers wandered into a field and couldn't see above the stalks. After searching through the night, their parents eventually found the two boys, who had taken shelter in an old wagon bed. It's not so different for us as adults. While we're experiencing the beauty of the life we're in, we may wander into places we shouldn't go. We become lost, not able to see above the distractions around us. Have you lost your way lately? Maybe you've gotten into something that once seemed like fun but is now confusing and threatening. Know that your Father God is searching for you. He's calling your name. He will rescue you, take you in his arms, and carry you home.

What man of you, having a hundred sheep, if he loses one of them, does not leave the ninety-nine in the wilderness, and go after the one which is lost until he finds it? And when he has found it, he lays it on his shoulders, rejoicing. And when he comes home, he calls together his friends and neighbors, saying to them, "Rejoice with me, for I have found my sheep which was lost!"

LUKE 15:4-6

When you're lost in those woods, it sometimes takes you a while to realize that you are lost.

ELIZABETH GILBERT, *EAT PRAY LOVE*

What other people think of you is none of your business.

AMISH PROVERB

The Eyes of Others

The Amish have a charming, slightly off-kilter view of life. Often it's expressed in a phrase or a quaint saying that reveals something profound in a very simple package. So it is with this little proverb, which highlights the reality that many of us measure ourselves based on the opinions of others. Is this true for you too? Yet the Amish say that what others think about you is none of *your* beeswax. In other words, it's not only unhealthy for you to preoccupy your mind with what others think but also a waste of time. As is often the case, the Amish echo the wisdom of the Bible, which tell us to "keep our eyes fixed on Jesus" (Hebrews 12:2, GNT) and "be anxious for nothing" (Philippians 4:6). God wants you to relax and stop wasting time fretting about what others think. Focus instead on the business that God has for you today.

It is dangerous to be concerned with
what others think of you, but
if you trust the Lord, you are safe.

PROVERBS 29:25, GNT

A Fish Tale

In one episode of *Little House on the Prairie*, a man named Ebenezer Sprague is sitting on a log, his fishing line in the pond, with nary a fish caught. Laura sits nearby and catches several fish with her special bait. When she offers some to Ebenezer, he insists that, according to the many books he has read, he's using the correct lure. Laura amusingly points out that perhaps the problem is "the fish just haven't read the books." Sometimes we've read the manual, but the computer still doesn't work. Sometimes we've studied the installation instructions, but the door still doesn't fit the doorway. Falling down along the way—suffering failure, even when we think we're doing things right—is not only common but also important. It's how we learn and grow. The Amish have a saying: "Learn from your failures, or you will fail to learn." Perhaps you're struggling with a recent setback. Rather than get down on yourself, turn the situation over to God. Let him use it to do a mighty work in your life. Through your weakness, he will lead you into a season of fresh accomplishments.

I will boast all the more gladly about my weaknesses, so that
Christ's power may rest on me. That is why, for Christ's sake,
I delight in weaknesses, in insults, in hardships, in persecutions,
in difficulties. For when I am weak, then I am strong.

2 CORINTHIANS 12:9-10, NIV

*If you wish
to be happy,
we'll tell you
the way:
don't live
tomorrow
till you've lived
today.*

AMISH PROVERB

A Time to Be Born and a Time to Die

Most people know the phrase "A time to be born, a time to die" from the sixties pop song "Turn! Turn! Turn!" by The Byrds. Many farmers also recognize the Bible as the original source of the lyrics, taken from chapter 3 of the book of Ecclesiastes. The passage eloquently expresses the beauty and purposes of life's different seasons, and countryfolk see many of these aspects played out in the cycle of farm life. Some of us, however, fail to pay attention to the message later in the chapter—that God wants us to "be happy and to do good" and to "find satisfaction" in our work (NIV). Consider taking time right now to embrace the moment you're in. Thank God for what he has given you in this season of life. Praise him for what is good and beautiful in your world today.

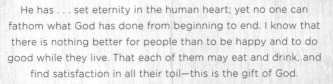

He has . . . set eternity in the human heart; yet no one can fathom what God has done from beginning to end. I know that there is nothing better for people than to be happy and to do good while they live. That each of them may eat and drink, and find satisfaction in all their toil—this is the gift of God.

ECCLESIASTES 3:11-13, NIV

Dying on the Inside

The 1985 science fiction film *Brazil* presents a devastating picture of an urban life in which people are consumed by corporate industrial jobs that keep them trapped in a meaningless existence. They have been stripped of hope and are slowly dying on the inside. Is this how you feel sometimes about your work and your life? Has a relentless day-after-day routine numbed you to the sweetness of life? A weekend in the country might do you a world of good. Even better would be a weekend retreat with the Lord. Take some time to plan a getaway where you can let your tears flow while you talk with him about the despair in your life. Tell him you're dying on the inside, and ask him to restore your soul.

Have compassion on me, LORD, for I am weak. Heal me, LORD, for my bones are in agony. I am sick at heart. . . . I am worn out from sobbing. All night I flood my bed with weeping, drenching it with my tears.

PSALM 6:2-3, 6, NLT

I waited patiently for the LORD to help me, and he turned to me and heard my cry. He lifted me out of the pit of despair, out of the mud and the mire. He set my feet on solid ground and steadied me as I walked along. He has given me a new song to sing, a hymn of praise to our God.

PSALM 40:1-3, NLT

Running through the Side of a Barn

Remember the time Jesus was speaking to a crowd so thick that some men took extraordinary measures to ensure their paralyzed friend's healing? The throng of people were like the side of a barn—the men couldn't get through them to carry their friend to Jesus. So they climbed up to the roof, cut a hole in it, and lowered the stretcher into the room where Jesus was preaching. Jesus forgave the man's sins and healed him! Jesus can take your problems, too, and transform them into breakthroughs. Maybe you're facing something that seems insurmountable—a challenge at work or a difficult relationship. What barn wall blocks you these days? Know that Jesus breaks down walls and welcomes those who come to him in unconventional ways. With Jesus, where there's a wall, there's a way.

[Jesus] said to the man, "I tell you, get up, take your mat and go home." He got up, took his mat and walked out in full view of them all. This amazed everyone and they praised God, saying, "We have never seen anything like this!"

MARK 2:10-12, NIV

If you had faith even as small as a mustard seed, you could say to this mountain, "Move from here to there," and it would move. Nothing would be impossible.

MATTHEW 17:20, NLT

Every miracle Jesus does starts with a problem.

AMISH PROVERB

God's blessing
gained
is all
obtained.

PENNSYLVANIA
GERMAN PROVERB

Produce Stand

At a roadside stand, the fruit of a farmer's labor is shared: baskets of freshly harvested tomatoes, cucumbers, onions, cherries, and sweet corn atop a red-and-white checkered tablecloth. A simple yet profound image: piles of produce—evidence of God's abundant blessing—sold to strangers with pride and pleasure. It is the farmer saying, "See what God has done through my labor!" What are you—through your life—offering to those around you? How is your presence a produce stand of God's blessing? Today think about sharing some of the crop of goodness and grace God has grown in you.

The LORD will grant you plenty of goods, in the fruit of your body, in the increase of your livestock, and in the produce of your ground, in the land of which the LORD swore to your fathers to give you. The LORD will open to you His good treasure, the heavens, to give the rain to your land in its season, and to bless all the work of your hand.

DEUTERONOMY 28:11-12

What Are You Living For?

We would do well to reflect on our lives more often. Whether we're from the country, city, or suburbs, we can get caught up in jobs, errands, and events with family and friends, rolling from day to day without taking stock of ourselves. Over time, we lose our purpose. Take a moment, if you can, and find a place where you can touch God's good world—a perch in a park, a footpath in a forest, a seat in front of a sunrise or sunset. Let God's nature inspire you to think, ponder, and reflect. Ask yourself, *What am I living for?* The Bible tells us that the only way we will truly be complete is to live for Christ. If you are already a follower of Jesus, perhaps you have forgotten to keep him at the center of your life. If you are not a follower of Jesus, consider becoming one—what he offers is not religion but a life filled with meaning and direction.

For to me, to live is Christ, and to die is gain.

PHILIPPIANS 1:21

The "Different" Life

City folk often don't understand life on the farm. To them, rural living seems hard—nothing is convenient, and sometimes you even need to make your meals from scratch. "It's just really different," they say. Of course, the difference of country living is exactly the beauty of it. So is a life devoted to God. It sets you apart. Makes you different. It sometimes causes others to scratch their heads and look at you sideways. No, following God isn't easy or convenient. But it not only makes you different but also *makes a difference*. Living in the perfect will of God puts you in a place where you can influence others for good. So today, embrace the life others don't understand. Walk through your day with God, step-by-step. Know that the difference of the God-life is exactly the beauty of it.

Do not be conformed to this world, but be transformed
by the renewing of your mind, that you may prove what is
that good and acceptable and perfect will of God.

ROMANS 12:2

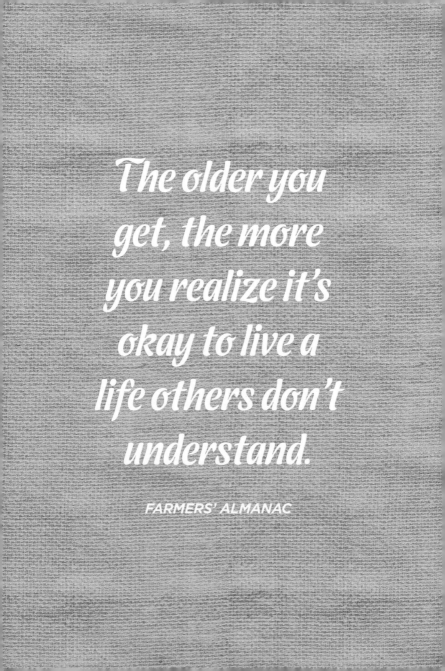

The older you get, the more you realize it's okay to live a life others don't understand.

FARMERS' ALMANAC

Synchronicity

It's early June, and you're at Great Smoky Mountains National Park. You won a lottery pass to be one of a thousand people to see the annual show—the amazing performance of synchronous fireflies. You're treated to behold not only an unusual abundance of fireflies but also, gradually, the fireflies blinking in unison. This is their means of communication with each other—their small individual lights synchronizing to make brilliant pulses in the night sky. One may wonder if this isn't also what pleases God as he looks upon us. We each have our own light to shine, communicating God's love; but when our lights sync with the lights of others, a spectacular show of praise and worship is released. Today, if you are a bit discouraged about your own life, feeling down about your significance in this world, think about the synchronous fireflies. Know that your light matters—especially because you're not alone.

You are the light of the world. A city set on a hill cannot be hidden. Nor do people light a lamp and put it under a basket, but on a stand, and it gives light to all in the house. In the same way, let your light shine before others, so that they may see your good works and give glory to your Father who is in heaven.

MATTHEW 5:14-16, ESV

God's Country

The story goes that an old farmer was on his porch talking with a visitor when somehow they started talking about God. The visitor, rather full of himself, said, "I don't believe in God—you can't prove his existence." The wise farmer said nothing but turned and looked out beyond the farmyard. There before them were fields of growing crops, a thriving green woodland, and a wide expanse of deep-blue sky. The visitor, noticing the farmer's gaze, took in this landscape of God's handiwork and started to understand the old man's point. "Oh," he simply said. Sometimes we get so wrapped up in our own issues that we lose sight of God's presence in our lives and in the world. Perhaps you have been self-focused and inwardly preoccupied. Remember that the heavens proclaim the glory of God. He's right here with us—you just need to look up.

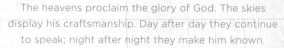

The heavens proclaim the glory of God. The skies
display his craftsmanship. Day after day they continue
to speak; night after night they make him known.

PSALM 19:1-2, NLT

The country soothes us, refreshes us, lifts us up with religious suggestion.

EDWIN HUBBEL CHAPIN,
MORAL ASPECTS OF CITY LIFE

Keep calm
and
bake bread.

AUTHOR UNKNOWN

Friendship Bread

Amish Friendship Bread is yummy, but the real deal of it is not the recipe. The making of Friendship Bread involves a social process. First, a humble jar of sourdough starter—enough to bake the bread and more to give away—is cultivated, and the starter gets passed along to a friend and then to a friend of that friend, and on and on. It's the "chain letter" of cooking. In spiritual terms, it might remind you of the old campfire song "Pass It On" or the practice of everyone lighting candles at Christmas Eve service to the tune of "Silent Night." Now think of yourself as the starter. Cultivate thoughts of all that God has done for you and let them grow within. Then tell others—give some of that deliciousness to people around you so they may likewise cultivate, grow, and share the amazing goodness of God, the Bread of Life.

We will not hide them from their children, telling to the generation to come the praises of the LORD, and His strength and His wonderful works that He has done.

PSALM 78:4

Jesus said to them, "I am the bread of life. He who comes to Me shall never hunger."

JOHN 6:35

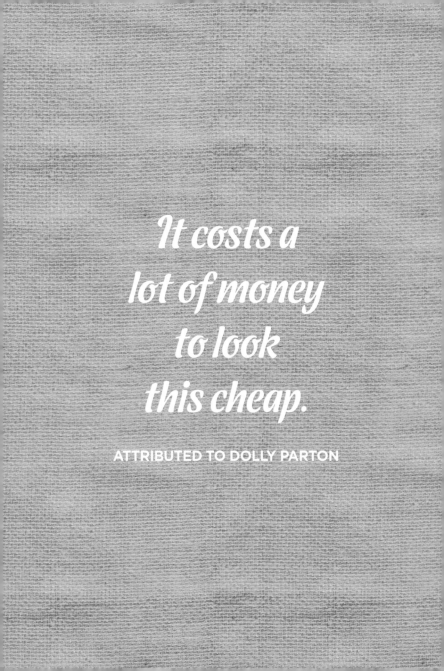

*It costs a
lot of money
to look
this cheap.*

ATTRIBUTED TO DOLLY PARTON

Keeping It Real

The culture of "country"—its music, style, clothing, and other trappings—projects a sense of authenticity. It celebrates the farming life and proudly embraces all that is informal, down-home, and real. Yet although we market ourselves as authentic, we sometimes still strive to look like the Christians we really aren't. Research professor Brené Brown says, "Authenticity is the daily practice of letting go of who we think we're supposed to be and embracing who we are." In fact, the Bible tells us that being a Christian is actually about admitting our failures and brokenness. But it doesn't stop there: It's also about letting God accept us as we are and believing he will finish the good work he started—until one day we perfectly reflect his righteous character. Perhaps you may want to consider dropping your mask. God knows your sins and weaknesses and loves you anyway. Enjoy the freedom of keeping it real by living as your authentic self.

Since you have heard about Jesus and have learned the truth that comes from him, throw off your old sinful nature and your former way of life, which is corrupted by lust and deception. Instead, let the Spirit renew your thoughts and attitudes. Put on your new nature, created to be like God—truly righteous and holy.

EPHESIANS 4:21-24, NLT

Go Fly a Kite

On a sunny day, without anything else in the world to do, a young'un races across a field, string in hand, and her kite catches the breeze, lifting into the air. The image of a child flying a kite is a picture of freedom—a beautiful representation of how God's breath of life lifts our kites—our lives—even higher. With God's presence in our lives, we can fly beyond our helpless, earthbound circumstances. If you feel stuck in the miry clay, perhaps it's time to fly a kite. Ask God to lift you up, to release your boots from the mud, and to help you soar once again.

The LORD . . . brought me up out of a horrible pit, out of the miry clay, and set my feet upon a rock, and established my steps. He has put a new song in my mouth—praise to our God; many will see it and fear, and will trust in the LORD.

PSALM 40:1-3

Those who wait on the LORD shall renew their strength; they shall mount up with wings like eagles, they shall run and not be weary, they shall walk and not faint.

ISAIAH 40:31

*True courage
is like a kite;
a contrary wind
raises it higher.*

ATTRIBUTED TO
JEAN ANTOINE PETIT-SENN

More Is Less

If you spend much time in a country kitchen, there's a good chance you've used an abundance of cooking utensils: the avocado slicer, the strawberry huller, the garlic chopper, the butter cutter . . . and in another drawer, perhaps, you've stashed away a pancake pen and herb scissors. Each gadget promises to make life easier. Of course, when you are finally ready to use, say, the cheese gun, you never quite know where it is. Your kitchen is all a-clutter with stuff you don't really need. Actually, a paring knife does just fine for most jobs, right? You may want to ask, *Does this present a similar picture of my life today?* Are you weighed down with so much stuff—possessions, worries, people, to-dos—that you've become paralyzed to the point of not being able to cook up anything at all? Consider paring it all down to the only thing that matters: your relationship with God. Focus on that. God is abundantly more than everything else put together.

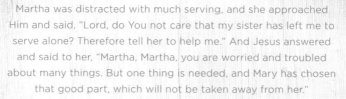

Martha was distracted with much serving, and she approached Him and said, "Lord, do You not care that my sister has left me to serve alone? Therefore tell her to help me." And Jesus answered and said to her, "Martha, Martha, you are worried and troubled about many things. But one thing is needed, and Mary has chosen that good part, which will not be taken away from her."

LUKE 10:40-42

The Way, the Truth, and the Life

What city folk often don't understand is that country living isn't just a place or an agricultural profession but also a rhythm of work and play—a cycle of birth and bud, green and growth, ripening and harvest, fallow and resting. It often connects a person to the roots of life in ways that others have lost touch with. In the same way, being a Christian isn't about being religious or just doing good; it's about following Jesus in everything a person does: a cycle of dying to self, rebirth, and spiritual growth. Jesus connects us to true life in ways we have never known.

Thomas said to Him, "Lord, we do not know where You are going, and how can we know the way?" Jesus said to him, "I am the way, the truth, and the life. No one comes to the Father except through Me."

JOHN 14:5-6

I beseech you therefore, brethren, by the mercies of God, that you present your bodies a living sacrifice, holy, acceptable to God, which is your reasonable service.

ROMANS 12:1

Farming is more than a job; it is a way of life.

LYMAN BRYSON,
"CAN THE FARMER BE SAVED?"

The Beauty of Broken

Every week, we head off to church all fixed up in our best duds. One argument for wearing nice clothes to church is that doing so honors God. A fair point, but God knows that "handsome" or "pretty" doesn't really cover the brokenness we each have inside. But to him, the problem is not that we are broken; it's that we try to hide it. In fact, it's only when we acknowledge our brokenness to him that he is able to work his miraculous purposes in and through us. Author Elisa Morgan says, "Brokenness is nothing to be ashamed of. It's nothing to hide. . . . Our brokenness doesn't disqualify us, but qualifies us." It puts us on God's list of works in progress, masterpieces he's in the process of restoring. So go ahead and wear your Sabbath best, but don't wear it as a disguise. Open up to the Lord about your brokenness, and be real about it with others too. Let them see the great work God is doing in you.

The sacrifice you desire is a broken spirit. You will not reject a broken and repentant heart, O God.

PSALM 51:17, NLT

We are God's masterpiece. He has created us anew in Christ Jesus, so we can do the good things he planned for us long ago.

EPHESIANS 2:10, NLT

It was such a pleasure to sink one's hands into the warm earth, to feel at one's fingertips the possibilities of the new season.

KATE MORTON,
THE FORGOTTEN GARDEN

Touching God's Good Earth

Scientists have proven that gardening is good for our health because it stimulates serotonin—the "happy" chemical that helps people overcome depression and bolster their immune systems. Sinking our hands into warm, moist earth gives us contact with a particular bacteria that triggers the release of serotonin in our brains. Even before the science proved it, countryfolk have known the joys of being connected to nature and plunging hands and feet into God's good earth. But if we don't live in the country, or if we do and forget to appreciate it, over time we might become separated from the joys and benefits of direct connection with God's creation. You don't need to have a green thumb or a garden to dig into warm soil; consider taking a walk in the woods or spending some time at a nature preserve. Simply enjoy smelling and touching the rich, loamy soil. Also ask God for the "good soil" of a humble, wise heart so he can multiply the good things he has planted in your life "a hundred times more" (Luke 8:8, NIV).

Before the mountains were formed, before
the hills, [wisdom] was born—before he had made
the earth and fields and the first handfuls of soil.

PROVERBS 8:25-26, NLT

Gardening by the Moon

It's become the new thing. You might call it a fad, although it's been around for millennia. "Gardening by the moon" is the practice of cultivating plants in sync with specific phases of the lunar cycle. As the *Farmers' Almanac* explains, it's "a philosophy of working with, rather than against nature." That's not a bad way of thinking about life. How often do we plow forward day by day without thinking about God, the very creator of nature, or about his plans and purposes for us? When we plant our life-garden *our* way, growth is often stymied and success limited. We never become beautiful in the way we could be—God's way. It's best to align ourselves with the one who created the moon—who created each of us. Will you work with, and not against, the one who planted the garden of your life?

The Lord God took the man and put him in the
garden of Eden to tend and keep it.

GENESIS 2:15

One is nearer
God's heart
in a garden than
anywhere else
on earth.

DOROTHY FRANCES GURNEY,
"GOD'S GARDEN"

The Powers of Flowers

Gardening can be a kind of time travel, reminding us of something from the past while also pointing us to a beautiful future. The fragrance of a hyacinth or the particular pink of a peony might bring back the memory of a loved one, and a seed laid in the ground and covered gently with topsoil carries the promise of a time to come. Likewise, a gift of flowers to those in bereavement acknowledges both the loss of their loved one and the hope of heaven. What hopes do you have for tomorrow? What are the bright, fragrant flowers in your life pointing to the future? Think about what God has promised, what he has in store for you, and the bouquet he has given to remind you of his beautiful plans.

Even the wilderness and desert will be glad in those days. The wasteland will rejoice and blossom with spring crocuses. Yes, there will be an abundance of flowers and singing and joy! The deserts will become as green as the mountains of Lebanon, as lovely as Mount Carmel or the plain of Sharon. There the LORD will display his glory, the splendor of our God.

ISAIAH 35:1-2, NLT

Warm familiar scents drift softly from the oven, and imprint forever upon our hearts that this is home and that we are loved.

ARLENE STAFFORD-WILSON,
LANARK COUNTY CALENDAR

An Open Home

A farm home is a hub of activity—family, friends, and farmhands coming and going, sharing conversations and meals after breaking from the rhythm of hard work. You wouldn't want it any other way, would you? Living close to the land, you know that hospitality—a welcoming environment with plenty of hearty food—is key to caring for the people who tend the ground and livestock God has given you. As such, you want them to partake of the comforts and sweet aromas of *home*. In a way, the Bible is the story of God coming home to us. Sounds strange to think of God that way, but the Bible tells us so: "The Word [Jesus Christ] became human and made his home among us" (John 1:14, NLT). It also talks about him making his home in our hearts. The question is whether the home of our hearts is open to him. Today, take a look at your spiritual home. Perhaps lately its door has been shut to the presence of God. Take some time right now to ask him to rekindle a fire in your heart for him.

Christ will make his home in your hearts as
you trust in him. Your roots will grow down
into God's love and keep you strong.

EPHESIANS 3:17, NLT

The Worth of Water

Farmers today have updated systems and technologies for providing water to their crops—especially during seasons of extreme dryness, when rain does not come. As Ben Franklin said, "When the well's dry, we know the worth of water." However the water is routed and delivered, ultimately it must come from heaven, just as our own spiritual refreshment does. Have you been feeling dry—spiritually dry—during this season of your life? A good place to go for "spiritual irrigation" is the book of Psalms. David, who wrote many of the Psalms, was considered "a man after [God's] own heart" (1 Samuel 13:14), and yet he struggled with dry times when he despaired deeply and felt distant from God. But he was a man of faith who turned to God again and again so that living water could drench his soul. Go to the Bible, and find a kindred soul in David. Ask God to shower you with his blessings.

O LORD, how long will you forget me? Forever? How long will you look the other way? How long must I struggle with anguish in my soul, with sorrow in my heart every day?

PSALM 13:1-2, NLT

I trust in your unfailing love. I will rejoice because you have rescued me. I will sing to the LORD because he is good to me.

PSALM 13:5-6, NLT

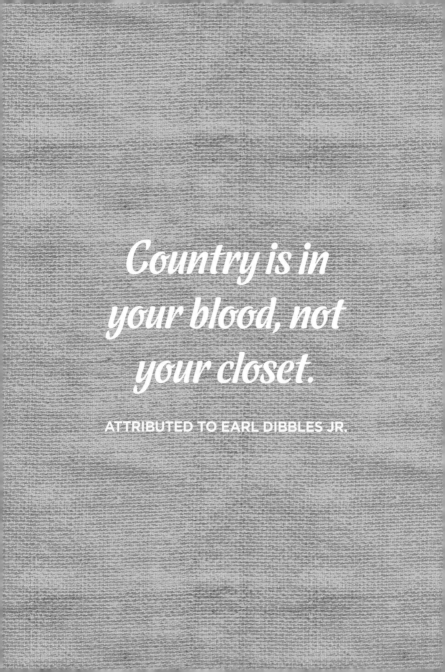

Country is in your blood, not your closet.

ATTRIBUTED TO EARL DIBBLES JR.

True-Blue Jeans

There is, surprisingly, a brand of furniture paint—and furniture to go with it—that claims to be "country chic." Some stores also sell country chic linens and dinnerware. Country chic clothing—stylish jeans, boots, and flannel shirts—are in vogue as well, although authentic countryfolk would never say the words *in vogue*, and true-blue country jeans are actually worn out, dusty, and smudged with mud. This question of what is real and authentic also suggests a spiritual question: In your Christian life, are you really who you claim to be? Is your faith hanging in a closet but not really running in your blood? Is your faith true-blue, properly smudged by being lived out in real life with people around you? Why not take time today and examine yourself before God. Ask him how you can make your faith less "Christian chic" and more authentic, more present in the lives of others.

Don't just pretend to love others. Really love them. Hate what is wrong. Hold tightly to what is good. Love each other with genuine affection, and take delight in honoring each other. Never be lazy, but work hard and serve the Lord enthusiastically. Rejoice in our confident hope. Be patient in trouble, and keep on praying. When God's people are in need, be ready to help them. Always be eager to practice hospitality.

ROMANS 12:9-13, NLT

Dream Again

There's a good gospel song by James Fortune titled "Dream Again." The lyrics speak to those who have experienced disappointments and roadblocks in life, even to the point of giving up. Perhaps this is your situation in life right now. Have you been faced with crushing discouragement? Have you given up on your dreams? The chorus of the song is a soaring call to "dream again." Understand that God can make things happen for you. With his help, you can revive your dreams once again. Try this today: Get in your car and start driving down an old country road. Take advantage of the time alone to talk to the Lord about your difficulties. Commit your plans to him, and prepare to watch him bring your dreams back to life.

Write the vision and make it plain on tablets,
that he may run who reads it. For the vision is yet
for an appointed time; but at the end it will speak,
and it will not lie. Though it tarries, wait for it;
because it will surely come, it will not tarry.

HABAKKUK 2:2-3

God made old country roads for driving and dreaming.

TIM McGRAW,
"TWO LANES OF FREEDOM"

Jesus Is in the Room

The Amish have a reputation for being quiet and reserved. So when it comes to this Amish saying—"When you speak, always remember that God is one of your listeners"—we might think, *That's easy for them to say!* For the rest of us, our speech is harder to control. But what if we were to take this proverb to heart? What if we approached our conversations with others as if Jesus were right there listening? In fact, he is. He sees and hears our interactions with family, friends, and coworkers. How would we speak differently if we fully realized this truth? Would we give vent to our anger or impatience or hurtful remarks? Probably not. Today, imagine Jesus there with you in the presence of others, listening. See how that changes you, your dialogue, your relationships—and even how you come privately to God in prayer.

Those who guard their lips preserve their lives,
but those who speak rashly will come to ruin.

PROVERBS 13:3, NIV

Let no corrupting talk come out of your mouths, but
only such as is good for building up, as fits the occasion,
that it may give grace to those who hear.

EPHESIANS 4:29, ESV

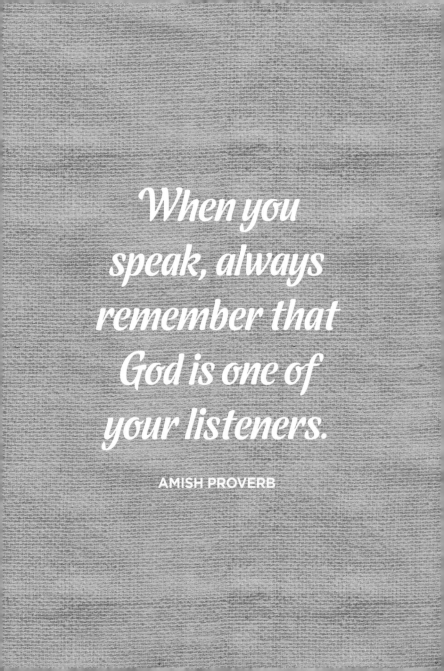

When you speak, always remember that God is one of your listeners.

AMISH PROVERB

In order to
mold his people,
God often has
to melt them.

AMISH PROVERB

The State of Butter

The country cook knows that when baking with butter, it must take just the right form. Piecrust requires butter that is cold and crumbly. The best cookies need butter that's soft and can be creamed with sugar. Quick breads and brownies often turn out best with melted butter. The state of the butter makes a difference in how your recipe holds up. Likewise, your own state of being affects the quality of your life and the lives of those around you. If you're facing challenges, trials, and hard times, maybe this is the result of God softening you a little. Perhaps he is working in your life to shape you into the form where you will be most useful to his work in the world. Today, spend some time in prayer about these things. Ask the Lord to reveal to you the purposes for his divine chemistry in your life.

O LORD, you are our Father.
We are the clay, and you are the potter.
We all are formed by your hand.

ISAIAH 64:8, NLT

Shall what is formed say to the one who
formed it, "You did not make me"? Can the pot
say to the potter, "You know nothing"?

ISAIAH 29:16, NIV

Getting to Know You

Do you have a special place where you like to be alone with God? Sometimes the countryside is the best option. In a landscape of rich forests or fertile fields, of flat or rolling terrain and wide horizons, you can feel as if you are face-to-face with God himself. Of course, you can also talk with him at any time and in any place, but do you? Perhaps you have been too busy lately. Pick a special spot in the country and get away to be with him. Bathe yourself in the gorgeousness he created, spend time in prayer and the Word of God, and get to know the God who loves you.

The people who know their God will be strong.

DANIEL 11:32, NLT

I pray for you constantly, asking God, the glorious
Father of our Lord Jesus Christ, to give you spiritual wisdom
and insight so that you might grow in your knowledge of God.
I pray that your hearts will be flooded with light so that you can
understand the confident hope he has given to those he called—
his holy people who are his rich and glorious inheritance.

EPHESIANS 1:16-18, NLT

I roamed the countryside searching for answers to things I did not understand.

LEONARDO DA VINCI

The Mystery of Wind

Tornadoes left their damaging imprint on Plainfield, Illinois, in 1974 and 1984, and just six years later, another tornado violently leveled much of the town, killing twenty-eight people. You would think the residents of Plainfield would have simply given up. Instead, they rebuilt and restored their community. In life there are often hard winds that shake us. When a tornado rips through our lives, we don't understand why—the winds of life are mysteries. What's the tornado in your life right now? It's easy to trust in God when you're going through good times, but not so much when strong winds are a-blowin'. Right now you are called to stand strong while your faith is being tested. Consider this an important moment to pray, to hear God's voice through his Word, and to believe firmly that he will care for you.

Whoever hears these sayings of Mine, and does them, I will liken him to a wise man who built his house on the rock: and the rain descended, the floods came, and the winds blew and beat on that house; and it did not fall, for it was founded on the rock.

MATTHEW 7:24-25

My brethren, count it all joy when you fall into various trials, knowing that the testing of your faith produces patience. But let patience have its perfect work, that you may be perfect and complete, lacking nothing.

JAMES 1:2-4

The Glory of Grain Dust

During the wheat harvest, when the sun is at just the right angle in the late afternoon sky, one can often see flecks of shimmering glitter in the waning light. This is the glory of grain dust—and also a reminder to us of God's work of creation. The Bible says that he made human beings out of mere dust. He took the primal stuff of existence and fashioned each of us according to his image, displaying us on the world's stage with glitter and glimmer. Today, think on this: God creates beautiful things out of dust—even the dust of our failures. Come to him in prayer and ask him how you can dazzle your world.

The LORD God formed man of the dust of the
ground, and breathed into his nostrils the breath
of life; and man became a living soul.

GENESIS 2:7, KJV

When I consider Your heavens, the work of Your fingers,
the moon and the stars, which You have ordained, what is man that
You are mindful of him? . . . For You have made him a little lower
than the angels, and You have crowned him with glory and honor.

PSALM 8:3-5

Country Quiet

What's that noise in your life today? What voices are screaming, and what background thrum is adding to the volume: Kids? Work? The complications of life? Consider escaping the rat race for a few days at a small-town B and B or a country inn. Make your quiet getaway a time with God, for even Jesus did this. After days of preaching to growing crowds, enduring the noise of multitudes, he found a quiet spot where he could be alone and pray. Set aside the noise of the world, and treat yourself to time alone with your heavenly Father.

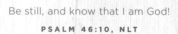

Be still, and know that I am God!

PSALM 46:10, NLT

Immediately Jesus made His disciples get into
the boat and go before Him to the other side, while
He sent the multitudes away. And when He had sent the
multitudes away, He went up on the mountain by Himself
to pray. Now when evening came, He was alone there.

MATTHEW 14:22-23

Give me, away, aside from the noise of the world, a rural domestic life.

WALT WHITMAN,
"GIVE ME THE SPLENDID SILENT SUN"

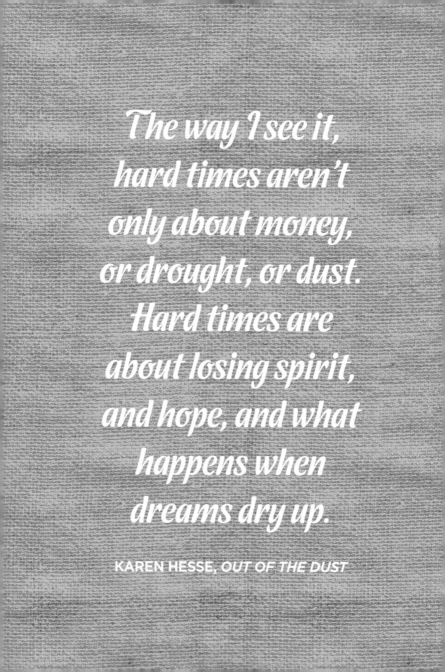

The way I see it,
hard times aren't
only about money,
or drought, or dust.
Hard times are
about losing spirit,
and hope, and what
happens when
dreams dry up.

KAREN HESSE, *OUT OF THE DUST*

The River of God

Some farmers say they would rather deal with a shortage of rain than a lack of sun, but of course the truth is that both are needed for healthy crops. Through modern irrigation methods, farmers have some control over dry spells by injecting water into their fields. But a full-on, long-term drought is deadly. When we go through spiritual droughts, sometimes we become so parched that we lose spirit and hope. Is this where you are in your journey? Your heavenly Father is there for you, providing just what you thirst for—spiritual irrigation for your soul. Spend time drinking in his presence through prayer, his Word, and fellowship with other believers. Allow him to water your life.

You take care of the earth and water it, making it rich and fertile. The river of God has plenty of water; it provides a bountiful harvest of grain, for you have ordered it so. You drench the plowed ground with rain, melting the clods and leveling the ridges. You soften the earth with showers and bless its abundant crops. You crown the year with a bountiful harvest; even the hard pathways overflow with abundance.

PSALM 65:9-11, NLT

They shall neither hunger nor thirst, neither heat nor sun shall strike them; for He who has mercy on them will lead them, even by the springs of water He will guide them.

ISAIAH 49:10

The Will to Thrive

There is photographic evidence of the struggle: A flower shooting up from a blanket of snow, its bloom unfolding in beautiful yellow petals in the late-winter sun. Another image of a lone cornstalk, growing in an empty field. A snapshot of a small azalea bush amid a dried-out, parched creek bed, proudly displaying its stark pink flowers and green foliage. Life struggles against all odds to grow and thrive. Does this describe your situation today? Are you struggling to keep things together? Do you feel overwhelmed and alone? This is an important time for you to turn to Jesus. He weathered the storms of life on earth just as you are now. Let him give you the strength to burst through this difficult time. He wants to give you the will not only to survive but also to thrive.

We have this treasure in earthen vessels, that the excellence
of the power may be of God and not of us. We are hard-pressed
on every side, yet not crushed; we are perplexed, but not in despair;
persecuted, but not forsaken; struck down, but not destroyed—
always carrying about in the body the dying of the Lord Jesus,
that the life of Jesus also may be manifested in our body.

2 CORINTHIANS 4:7-10

Dancing Shoes

The Shakers, a sect whose heyday was centuries ago, believed that dancing should be an important element of their worship—one of the reasons they were originally known as the "Shaking Quakers." "Lord of the Dance," a familiar country hymn based on an old Shaker tune, tells the story of Jesus' life, punctuated by a chorus that calls each of us to dance in joyous celebration of our Savior. Maybe you're plodding through a time in your life that feels heavy. And maybe this is an opportunity for you to answer that call to put on your dancing shoes. Think of the astonishing truth that God, through his Son, Jesus Christ, came to earth to deliver this world from the trauma of sin and death. The going may be tough, but God, in his grace, will carry you as you lean on his strength. As the song says, "Dance then, wherever you may be," and sing praises to the Lord for what he is doing in your life.

David danced before the LORD with all his might.

2 SAMUEL 6:14

The young women will dance for joy, and the men—old and young—will join in the celebration. I will turn their mourning into joy. I will comfort them and exchange their sorrow for rejoicing.

JEREMIAH 31:13, NLT

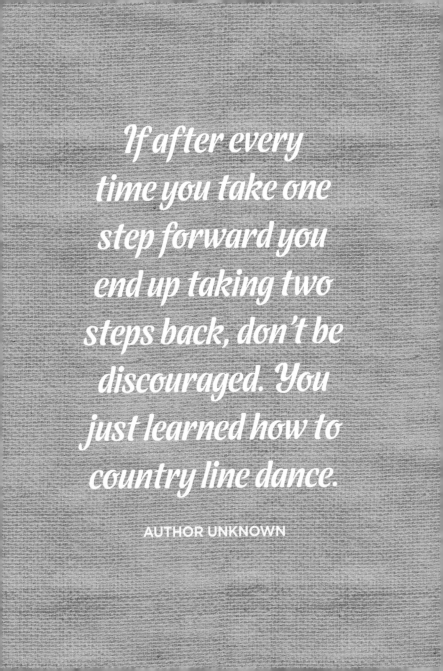

If after every time you take one step forward you end up taking two steps back, don't be discouraged. You just learned how to country line dance.

AUTHOR UNKNOWN

Blessings, Count 'Em

It's a Sunday night in August, and the air hangs hot and still. You're at church—a one-room, plain-as-pine sanctuary lined with hard wooden pews. Men from the country town have come in suits and ties, the women in skirts because "You gotta dress up for God; it's the right proper thing to do." Heat and hardwood—what's not to like? But this is the night for the hymn sing, when the week's woes fall away. The congregation breaks into singing, voices crescendoing on the first line of the refrain: "Count your blessings, name them one by one." It's important to let your work and worries fade into the background so you can think about all the ways God has blessed you. This is about finding the smiles in your life—not some forced spiritual practice. So yes, count your blessings. Make a list and name them one by one—and praise God for the wonders he has lavishly rained down on you.

Fix your thoughts on what is true, and honorable, and right, and pure, and lovely, and admirable. Think about things that are excellent and worthy of praise. Keep putting into practice all you learned and received from me—everything you heard from me and saw me doing. Then the God of peace will be with you.

PHILIPPIANS 4:8-9, NLT

Free to . . .

It's possible to drive through parts of Wyoming for miles and miles and never see another car. The state is a beautiful expanse of mountains and valleys—endless stretches of gorgeous land so sparsely populated that it seems like undiscovered territory. Just driving through, you can't help but develop a carefree spirit and wide-eyed wonder. You just feel free. In your life today, are you burdened by problems and conflicts? Of course, responsibilities are ever present, but perhaps you're shackled by something more substantial that keeps you in your own special prison. What is that for you right now? The Bible says that Christ died and rose to life so we could be set free. In him, sin—our own and the sins of others—no longer rules our lives. Perhaps something has crept back in and is keeping you from being truly free. Take some time to come to him in prayer. Ask for fresh forgiveness, for the ability to forgive others, and for the joyful freedom he offers.

It is for freedom that Christ has set us free.
Stand firm, then, and do not let yourselves be
burdened again by a yoke of slavery.

GALATIANS 5:1, NIV

This pure air braces the listless nerves, and warms the blood: I feel in freedom here.

JOANNA BAILLIE, *DE MONTFORT*

I always think of my sins when I weed. They grow apace in the same way and are harder still to get rid of.

HELENA RUTHERFURD ELY,
A WOMAN'S HARDY GARDEN

The Weeding Life

Gardeners will tell you that weeds seem to have a kind of evil intelligence—they know you're after them, so they cast their spores all over the place to make sure they stay alive. They are also programmed with a kind of "smart sense" to break off easily at the stem so the taproot remains behind—leaving sproutlings all over, ready to pop up again. Likewise, the weeds of our lives have an evil intelligence behind them: the crafty wiles of the enemy, who bars us from blossoming by seeding us with sin. The apostle Paul speaks of putting sin to death, essentially a process of weeding our own lives. It's time to take stock of the invasive species that are flourishing in our hearts. Do you know what your sins are and which corners they're hiding in? Time to get down on your knees and do some good, hard weeding.

Dear brothers and sisters, you have no obligation to do what your sinful nature urges you to do. For if you live by its dictates, you will die. But if through the power of the Spirit you put to death the deeds of your sinful nature, you will live. For all who are led by the Spirit of God are children of God.

ROMANS 8:12-14, NLT

Others hurled themselves into the water to escape the fire.

R. F. KUANG,
THE DRAGON REPUBLIC

Fire and Water

The beauty of the country belies the harshness of the weather. In 2013, in a beautiful rural area northeast of Colorado Springs, what is now known as the "Black Forest Fire" destroyed some fourteen thousand acres and nearly five hundred homes. No specific cause was ever identified, but the extreme heat and dry climate at the time fanned whatever spark might have occurred. In a similar fashion, we often don't know why sparks occur in our lives, resulting in blazing fires that cause hardship. Sometimes we feel puzzled and dejected, wondering why God doesn't intervene to prevent our difficulties. The truth is that his purposes are beyond our understanding. Are you facing the fire these days? The Bible reminds us that our troubles come disguised as opportunities for great joy. We need to train ourselves to allow the fires of our lives to bring us closer to God. It's during those times we most appreciate drinking deeply from the well of his cool, quenching, life-giving water.

Dear friends, don't be surprised at the fiery trials you are going through, as if something strange were happening to you. Instead, be very glad—for these trials make you partners with Christ in his suffering, so that you will have the wonderful joy of seeing his glory when it is revealed to all the world.

1 PETER 4:12-13

Pause

The rat race each day can be relentless, from that early morning alarm to the scramble into the work routine that tumbles into a day of chaos. And too often we carry our frantic busyness home with us into the evening and right into bedtime. No wonder we have trouble getting to sleep! If you don't have the benefit of spending a soothing spring night on a farmhouse porch, find a place of peace in your crazy life. Pull up a pillow, take a deep breath, and give it a rest—literally. Pause. Tell the Lord what's up by speaking aloud the big, pressing matters of your frantic day. One by one, drop your anxieties as you imagine yourself sitting at Jesus' feet, his gaze resting lovingly upon you. He will give you rest.

Come to me, all of you who are weary and carry
heavy burdens, and I will give you rest. Take my yoke upon
you. Let me teach you, because I am humble and gentle
at heart, and you will find rest for your souls. For my yoke
is easy to bear, and the burden I give you is light.

MATTHEW 11:28-30, NLT

Supper was cooked and eaten, the dishes washed, and darkness was falling softly on the prairie. No one wanted the lamp lighted, the spring night was so beautiful.

LAURA INGALLS WILDER,
BY THE SHORES OF SILVER LAKE

Good Grief

Some say it wasn't until they spent time living in the country that they began to understand the meaning of death. Surrounded by nature, every year they witness the cycle of life—the birth, growth, and death of plants and creatures. It's one thing when harvesting leads to the "death" of a field of cornstalks. When it's the death of a pet dog or prized rooster, it's much more personal. Sometimes loss takes other forms too. For you, it might be the death of a work project, canceled suddenly, or the death of a dream you've had for a long time. Maybe it is even the loss of a loved one—a friend or sister or parent. Knowing that death is part of the cycle of life doesn't ease your pain. Nothing can do that. Grief is something you simply have to live through. In a way, it's a good thing—coming to grips with life and death. But know this: God grieves with you. He hurts alongside you. Come to him in this season. Rest in him, and let him catch your tears.

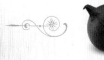

You keep track of all my sorrows. You have
collected all my tears in your bottle.

PSALM 56:8, NLT

The LORD is close to the brokenhearted and
saves those who are crushed in spirit.

PSALM 34:18, NIV

Barn Raising or Barn Razing?

Among the Amish, the entire community bands together when a barn needs to be built. Tools and supplies are ordered ahead of time, and teams are designated—it's an amazingly efficient process. In some cases, an entire barn is built in a single day. Sometimes a barn raising happens only after a barn "razing"—the tearing down of a structure that has decayed and deteriorated, outliving its value. Often in our lives old things must be *razed* before new things can be *raised*. If we hold on to old habits and unhealthy relationships beyond any point of value, sin creeps in and rots out the sacred spaces in our hearts. We are left feeling stuck, because we can't plan for something new until we take care of what's old. Have you allowed Jesus to tear down your deteriorated sin-life? You will never regret being raised up to an exciting God-fashioned life.

Everything—and I do mean everything—connected with that old way of life has to go. It's rotten through and through. Get rid of it! And then take on an entirely new way of life—a God-fashioned life, a life renewed from the inside and working itself into your conduct as God accurately reproduces his character in you.

EPHESIANS 4:22-24, MSG

The shop, the barn, the scullery, and the smithy become temples when men and women do all to the glory of God!

CHARLES SPURGEON, *MORNING AND EVENING*

Bathing in Green

A *Psychology Today* article talks about the mental health virtues of being in nature, noting that research has identified plenty of benefits from spending time in natural landscapes, or "bathing in green," as it's called. Countryfolk, of course, don't need PhDs to tell them what they've known all their lives: Living close to nature is good for your health. Likewise, God's Word tells us we should do some "Bible bathing." First Timothy 4:13, 15 says, "Devote yourself to the public reading of Scripture. . . . Practice these things, immerse yourself in them" (ESV). Here's an idea: Grab your Bible and travel to a place in the country where you can sit on a bench, a log, or a patch of grass. See how bathing in green and in God's Word at the same time will help you relax and hear God's voice. It will also green up your spirit and enrich your soul!

Christ . . . loved the church and gave Himself for her,
that He might sanctify and cleanse her with the washing
of water by the word, that He might present her to Himself
a glorious church, not having spot or wrinkle or any such
thing, but that she should be holy and without blemish.

EPHESIANS 5:25-27

The greatest glory in living lies not in never falling, but in rising every time we fall.

OLIVER GOLDSMITH

Tire Swing

Country and pop music legend Jimmy Buffett wrote a song titled "Life Is Just a Tire Swing." The lyrics recall his childhood memories of swinging in an old tire that hung from a rope attached to a tree. Maybe as a young child you had the same experience. Imagine you are a child again, this time being pushed by your father in a tire that hangs beside a pond. You shriek as you sail over the water, then feel safe again when you come back to your dad. Eventually you dare to let go and fall into the pond. The first time it's scary, but you know that your father will save you if needed. There's a spiritual lesson in this as well. God, your heavenly Father, protects you and keeps you safe. But when he sees you're living in a way that requires little faith, you may sense him challenging you to take a bigger risk so you'll learn to trust him more. Sometimes he wants you to jump into the pond.

Peter went over the side of the boat and walked on the water toward Jesus. But when he saw the strong wind and the waves, he was terrified and began to sink. "Save me, Lord!" he shouted. Jesus immediately reached out and grabbed him. "You have so little faith," Jesus said. "Why did you doubt me?"

MATTHEW 14:29-31, NLT

Name That Tune

Often songs have a twist—life was going along as usual, then something happened that changed everything. Country music almost always tells a story. The pleasure and power of its songs are often contained in stories of change. What is your life story? Is it a story of change, or is everything still the same ol', same ol'? Maybe you have resisted God's work in your life, choosing to hold on to private sins that grieve God's heart. Take time to imagine what a new page of your life could look like if you were pursuing God's will. With his help, find some different music and write yourself a new story, a new song.

Sing to the LORD a new song! For He
has done marvelous things; His right hand and
His holy arm have gained Him the victory.

PSALM 98:1

GOD rewrote the text of my life when I opened
the book of my heart to his eyes.

PSALM 18:24, MSG

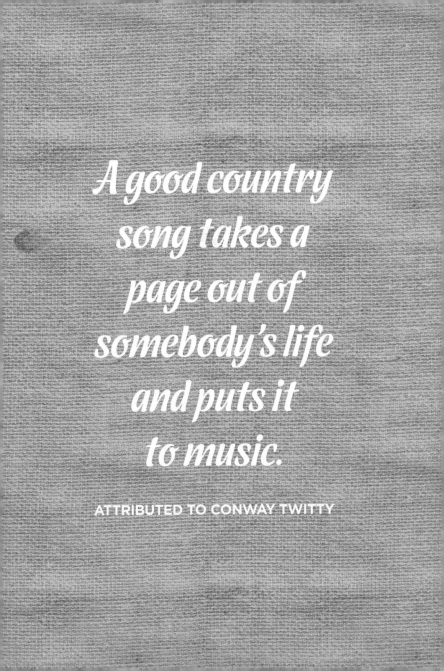

A good country
song takes a
page out of
somebody's life
and puts it
to music.

The Old Country Store

Outside the old country store stand two rusted gas pumps labeled "Esso." Inside, the old-fashioned freezer case is filled with Blue Bell ice cream, and MoonPies are stacked on the worn wooden front counter. Back in the day, folks would buy RC Cola to go with their MoonPies—the perfect comfort food combo. The old country store is a warm, nostalgic recollection for many. But God offers comfort food that's much more than a rosy memory. If you're in a strange place in life right now, a situation that feels unsettling, why not turn to God and ask him to ease your worries. Sit out on the porch with him. Let him comfort you with the finest food—the Bread of Life, Jesus. Today he offers you forgiveness for your sins; eternal life in the world to come; and peace, love, power, and joy to navigate the in-between.

Why spend your money on food that does not give you strength? Why pay for food that does you no good? Listen to me, and you will eat what is good. You will enjoy the finest food. Come to me with your ears wide open. Listen, and you will find life.

ISAIAH 55:2-3, NLT

"Comfort, yes, comfort My people!" says your God. . . . He will feed His flock like a shepherd; He will gather the lambs with His arm, and carry them in His bosom, and gently lead those who are with young.

ISAIAH 40:1, 11

These are a few of my favorite things.

"MY FAVORITE THINGS,"
THE SOUND OF MUSIC

Nehi Orange

Back in the day, it was common to pick up a Nehi Orange—or maybe a Nehi Grape—at the country store. Those flavors were standard, and hard-core Nehi fans may have had a hard time accepting the newfangled flavors that came later, like Nehi Blue Cream and Nehi Watermelon. Today at the country store, the vintage Nehi sign in the window reads, "Your favorite drink in your favorite flavor." What's *your* favorite Nehi flavor? Beyond that, what are some of your favorite everyday things? You could probably include at least "raindrops on roses and whiskers on kittens." But how about going a step further and naming your favorite things about God? How has he protected you? How has he provided for you? Make a list of God's wonderful works, and take time to praise him for his lavish, loving care—and all the fun ways he's flavored your life.

You have multiplied, O Lord my God, your wondrous deeds and your thoughts toward us; none can compare with you! I will proclaim and tell of them, yet they are more than can be told.

PSALM 40:5, ESV

Oh, that men would give thanks to the Lord for His goodness, and for His wonderful works to the children of men!

PSALM 107:31

"Follow Me"

Filling out an online application, a man pauses after the field "Occupation," then types in "Farmer." He sits back, smiles, and shakes his head. Being a farmer is so much more than an occupation. It's an upbringing, acres of land, and a homestead shared with your family—an entire culture in itself. There's another field on the form: "Religious affiliation." The man types "Christian," and yet he knows that being a Christian isn't just a label or an affiliation. Being a Christian is a radical way of life that requires giving up everything for Jesus. When Jesus said, "Follow me," you did. Reflect on that decision and examine your commitment to Jesus. Is it still fresh, or has it become fill-in-the-blank for you? Ask the Lord to renew your "first love" for him (Revelation 2:4).

As He walked by the Sea of Galilee, He saw Simon and Andrew his brother casting a net into the sea; for they were fishermen. Then Jesus said to them, "Follow Me, and I will make you become fishers of men." They immediately left their nets and followed Him.

MARK 1:16-18

I have been crucified with Christ; it is no longer I who live, but Christ lives in me; and the life which I now live in the flesh I live by faith in the Son of God, who loved me and gave Himself for me.

GALATIANS 2:20

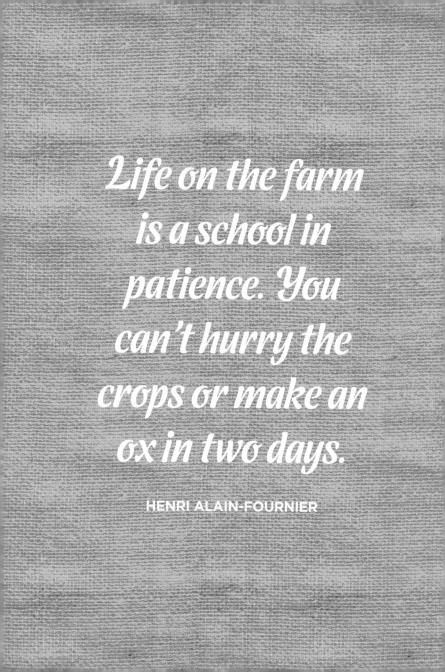

Life on the farm is a school in patience. You can't hurry the crops or make an ox in two days.

HENRI ALAIN-FOURNIER

Waiting Room

A fallow field is one that a farmer plows but does not seed. The soil is intentionally left unused for the purpose of replenishing its nutrients. It is made to wait for another season. A field that lies fallow is sometimes an apt image of our lives. If nothing significant appears to be happening, we feel stuck in a holding pattern, a waiting game. It seems we aren't getting any closer to our goals—even the purposes we believe God has for us. The Bible talks a lot about waiting and having patience during fallow times. It may be that in God's wisdom, we need downtime to replenish. Perhaps his timing is different from ours for the work he has for us to do. During these waiting seasons, one thing is certain: God wants us to spend more time with him. Think of fallow times in your life as opportunities to replenish your mind and heart.

I would have lost heart, unless I had believed that
I would see the goodness of the LORD in the land of the
living. Wait on the LORD; be of good courage, and He shall
strengthen your heart; wait, I say, on the LORD!

PSALM 27:13-14

I waited patiently for the LORD;
and He inclined to me, and heard my cry.

PSALM 40:1

The Joy of God's Smile

The movie *Chariots of Fire* features Olympic runner Eric Liddell saying, "I believe that God made me for a purpose . . . for China. But he also made me fast. And when I run, I feel his pleasure." Liddell won the gold medal in the 400 meters at the 1924 Summer Olympics. For him, being in the center of God's will, doing what he was made to do, was the sweet spot in which he felt God's smile. The Bible often uses the word *delight* in a way that we could also interpret as God's smile. God shows his delight in us in many ways. We might too easily overlook his smile in nature—how the changing seasons, the spreading sunsets, the golden fields of ripened wheat, and the budding green crops of corn, soybeans, and alfalfa are reflections of God's great grin. We might also miss God's smile in our daily lives if we're not living according to his purpose, pursuing his will. Maybe this is a good time to reflect on your life and realign yourself with God's purposes. God loves loves you. He wants to smile upon you. Live in his will, and start to feel his pleasure.

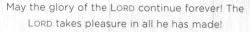

May the glory of the LORD continue forever! The LORD takes pleasure in all he has made!

PSALM 104:31, NLT

The LORD delights in his people; he crowns the humble with victory. Let the faithful rejoice that he honors them.

PSALM 149:4-5, NLT

Earth is here so kind, that just tickle her with a hoe and she laughs with a harvest.

BASIL IN DOUGLAS JERROLD'S
A MAN MADE OF MONEY

Vines and Branches

Japanese farmer Masanobu Fukuoka was famous—and controversial—for his minimalist approaches to farming. He advocated for natural cultivation and sparse human intervention. Fukuoka's philosophy was holistic—emphasizing that farming is about the cultivation of people just as much as the land and soil. Yet this isn't such a revolutionary idea; it's exactly what the Scriptures teach. Jesus often used agriculture as an image of God's work among his people. He likened himself to a grapevine, with his followers as the branches and his Father the gardener who carefully prunes us, the branches, so we will produce more abundant—and juicier—fruit. Take comfort in this. God is working in your heart, shaping you and pruning you to be more productive and successful.

I am the true grapevine, and my Father is the gardener. He cuts off every branch of mine that doesn't produce fruit, and he prunes the branches that do bear fruit so they will produce even more.

JOHN 15:1-2, NLT

"I will rebuke the devourer for your sakes, so that he will not destroy the fruit of your ground, nor shall the vine fail to bear fruit for you in the field," says the LORD of hosts.

MALACHI 3:11

The ultimate goal of farming is not the growing of crops, but the cultivation and perfection of human beings.

MASANOBU FUKUOKA,
THE ONE-STRAW REVOLUTION

He who kneels
before God
can stand before
any man.

ATTRIBUTED TO EZRA TAFT BENSON

Good Posture

Sometimes a certain picture graces the walls in country farm-houses—a rugged cowboy kneeling before the cross—a plaque bearing the words, "He who kneels before God can stand before anyone." The idea of someone strong and rugged humbling himself before God is powerful. It begs the question, What brought the cowboy to his knees? What brings you to *your* knees before the cross of Jesus? It may be that your everyday walk with the Lord makes you aware of your need for him, and kneeling is your frequent posture. But perhaps more often, like most of us, you have been humbled by recent events in your life, bringing you back into obedience to the Lord. If so, take some time now to come before Jesus. Kneel—physically get on your knees—and submit to him as your Lord. Ask him to forgive your pride in straying from him and to lead you in your future endeavors.

For this reason I kneel before the Father,
from whom every family
in heaven and on earth derives its name.

EPHESIANS 3:14-15, NIV

Ordinary Jane

For many years, newsman Bob Dotson was the host of the *Today* show segment titled "The American Story," featuring accounts of ordinary people doing extraordinary things. Dotson says, "Our country would be better served if we listened more to people who don't have titles in front of their names." In fact, America is carried on the backs of hardworking farmers, construction workers, and factory employees, as well as tireless moms and dads raising families. Yet our country tends to glorify the celebrity culture, and we get caught up in stargazing. Perhaps you compare yourself to others and question your worth in the world. Maybe you get discouraged because you're not famous or an expert at anything. Yet think about this: The people God most frequently uses to accomplish his will are ordinary Joes and Janes. You may not be famous or perceive yourself as important or skilled, but that makes you perfect for God's purposes. Rest in the assurance that although you may feel like no one special, God can and will accomplish great things through you.

Isn't it obvious that God deliberately chose men and women that the culture overlooks and exploits and abuses, chose these "nobodies" to expose the hollow pretensions of the "somebodies"?

1 CORINTHIANS 1:27-28, MSG

A good farmer is nothing more nor less than a handy man with a sense of humus.

E. B. WHITE

Humor Me

Crop farmers often have a quirky sense of humor, perhaps because they must. Their profession is utterly dependent on natural forces beyond their control, and looking at the bright side of life can help them stay sane. As Will Rogers purportedly remarked, "The farmer has to be an optimist or he wouldn't still be a farmer." As always, life is like farming—so many of our circumstances we cannot control. And yet, we strive hard to make things happen the way we want. Is this your life today? Are you anxious about that which you can't do anything about? Our efforts to maneuver outcomes are really about the struggle to trust God completely. You might do well to "let go and let God." Acknowledge your dependence on him, and believe that because of his great love for you, he will "work together for good" all that concerns you.

Blessed is the man who trusts in the LORD, and whose hope is the LORD. For he shall be like a tree planted by the waters, which spreads out its roots by the river, and will not fear when heat comes; but its leaf will be green, and will not be anxious in the year of drought, nor will cease from yielding fruit.

JEREMIAH 17:7-8

We know that all things work together for good to those who love God, to those who are the called according to His purpose.

ROMANS 8:28

A Time to Keep
and a Time to Throw Away

Recycling is a way of life for many people now, but farm families have been recycling longer than any of us, practicing an ecology of soil, resources, and water. And it's part of country culture to reuse that which still has value. But sometimes, farm folks will tell you, the house and farmyard can start to look like a secondhand store, teeming with piles of odds and ends. The time comes to just throw things away. Our lives can also become cluttered with useless stuff—the junk of past failures, troubled relationships, and old resentments. Should you think about about purging your life of all that weighs you down? Maybe you could make a list of your junkyard items. Consider asking God to remove them from your cluttered life. You'll feel lighter and freer once you take out the trash.

For everything there is a season, a time for every activity under heaven. . . . A time to keep and a time to throw away.

ECCLESIASTES 3:1, 6, NLT

Let all bitterness, wrath, anger, clamor, and evil speaking be put away from you, with all malice. And be kind to one another, tenderhearted, forgiving one another, even as God in Christ forgave you.

EPHESIANS 4:31-32

A Harvest of Souls

A farmer's harvest of crops they have labored over all year long depends on the seasons of winter, spring, summer, and fall cooperating to "do the right things" at the right times. Farmers watch the weather with the eyes of a hawk, knowing that too much rain here or not enough there will become a verdict on the yield at the end of the growing season. Ultimately they can't control the weather, of course; they must leave it in God's hands. In life, it's important to have that same trust and patience as well. We cannot evaluate our worth, our effectiveness, by measuring what gets produced each day or each week. This is all the more the case as we understand that our true "produce" is likely not found in the things we strive to achieve but in the people we interact with—children, loved ones, friends, even strangers we encounter who need a few kind words. Through our actions, we're sowing seeds of God's love in the lives of others. It will take a while to see them grow, however, so let's leave the harvest in God's hands.

Let us not become weary in doing good,
for at the proper time we will
reap a harvest if we do not give up.

GALATIANS 6:9, NIV

Judge each day not by the harvest you reap but by the seeds you plant.

WILLIAM ARTHUR WARD

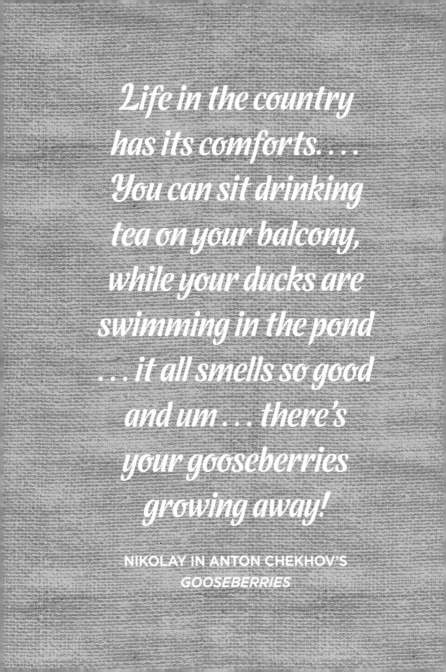

Life in the country
has its comforts. . . .
You can sit drinking
tea on your balcony,
while your ducks are
swimming in the pond
. . . it all smells so good
and um . . . there's
your gooseberries
growing away!

NIKOLAY IN ANTON CHEKHOV'S
GOOSEBERRIES

And There Are Gooseberries...

A country Thanksgiving is much like any Thanksgiving in the city—except that perhaps much of the food on the table has come directly from a garden or fields only yards away. Piled high on plates are wedges of squash, green bean casserole, corn pudding, and roasted turkey. Later there is pie, maybe made from pumpkins or apples grown right there on the farm. And then there are gooseberries: something more—the additional treat that God gives above and beyond. Thanksgiving is a celebration of the abundant blessings God so graciously bestows. He provides for us lavishly and surprisingly, sometimes to the point it seems too good to be true. Has your heavenly Father astonished you lately with his abundant blessings? How has he surprised you with his extravagance? Have you thanked him for that, praised him for all he has done for you?

God can pour on the blessings in astonishing ways so that you're ready
for anything and everything, more than just ready to do what needs
to be done. . . . This most generous God who gives seed to the farmer
that becomes bread for your meals is more than extravagant with you.
He gives you something you can then give away, which grows into
full-formed lives, robust in God, wealthy in every way, so that you can
be generous in every way, producing with us great praise to God.

2 CORINTHIANS 9:8-11, MSG

Freezing Fog

It's a rare but real weather phenomenon, a perfect storm of moist air meeting a cold front. It's called "freezing fog." The spectacle is beautiful—droplets crystallizing in midair, glistening in ground clouds, coating trees and fences. It's also dangerous, breaking branches and bringing down power lines. Sometimes in life we find ourselves in a perfect storm. Is that where you are today? Maybe you feel God has turned from you, leaving you in a cold front. It's so cold you feel like you're about to break. But could it be that it's time to come back to him? In this time of freezing life-fog, take a deep breath, and know that God will never leave you. Draw near to him.

By the breath of God ice is given,
and the broad waters are frozen. Also with
moisture He saturates the thick clouds.

JOB 37:10-11

I will cause breath to enter into you, and you shall live.

EZEKIEL 37:5

Born in a Barn

The phrase "born in a barn" is meant to be insulting, inferring that someone is ill-mannered, low-class, and of questionable heritage. Yet those who live on a farm with animals know the miracles of birth that happen in a barn. It is a miracle but no accident that Jesus himself was born among animals and placed in a manger rather than on a royal throne. He came to save all of us—not just the elite, or the rich, or the celebrity class. The good news of Christ's birth is that he was "born in a barn," the lowest of the low, to identify with those who have ordinary lives. If you ever get to a point where you doubt your standing in the world, turn your eyes upon Jesus—God as a human among us—who is your friend and Savior.

Though he was God, he did not think of equality with God as something to cling to. Instead, he gave up his divine privileges; he took the humble position of a slave and was born as a human being. When he appeared in human form, he humbled himself· in obedience to God and died a criminal's death on a cross.

PHILIPPIANS 2:6-8, NLT

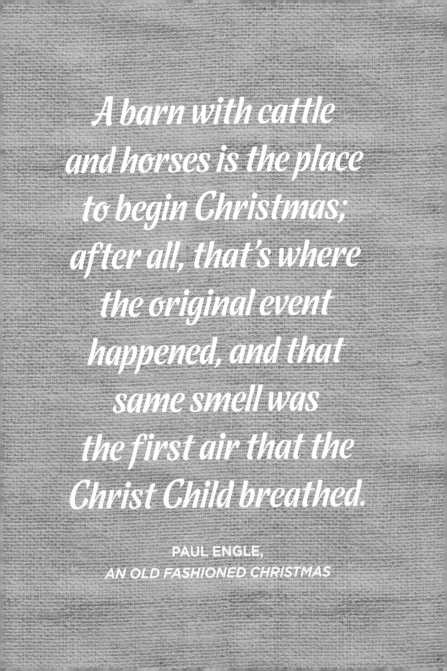

A barn with cattle and horses is the place to begin Christmas; after all, that's where the original event happened, and that same smell was the first air that the Christ Child breathed.

PAUL ENGLE,
AN OLD FASHIONED CHRISTMAS

The Sound of Hush

Did you know that in the bleak of winter, you can actually hear the snow falling? Snowflakes lighter than goose feathers somehow make a hushed sound as they float to the ground. As you look over the landscape, observing the dead remnants of harvest, perhaps the hills and fields are being covered in white. You might be reminded of the winters and little "deaths" you've endured in your own experience: the hurt of a dying friendship, failures at work, or the literal death of someone close. Life sometimes feels cold and hard. But the God who blankets the land with snow also creates the richness and beauty of each snowflake, providing water for the new life that lies ahead. So take heart and listen for the snow's hushed music . . . and make it the soundtrack of your life.

As the rain comes down, and the snow from heaven, and do not return there, but water the earth, and make it bring forth and bud, that it may give seed to the sower and bread to the eater, so shall My word be that goes forth from My mouth; it shall not return to Me void, but it shall accomplish what I please.

ISAIAH 55:10-11

Winter Wonderland

You might remember those days as a kid when you watched the TV weather guy in a loud sport coat predicting the season's first snowstorm. You would get excited at the prospect of sledding and making a snowman the next day if school was canceled. When the first flakes started to fall, you watched and marveled as the snow made all things new. The dusty, dirty landscape of dead November slowly transformed into a winter wonderland of white. Likewise, we sometimes get to a point in our lives when everything seems old and dead, when "all the leaves are brown." We feel trapped in the same old situations and the same old sins. We long for a snowstorm that will change our landscape. Thankfully, the Bible says that Christ wants to make our sins as white as snow. If we repent and turn our lives over to Jesus, all things become new. We can be made clean and white. Indeed, tomorrow can be a snow day!

"Come now, and let us reason together," says the LORD,
"though your sins are like scarlet, they shall be as white as snow;
though they are red like crimson, they shall be as wool."

ISAIAH 1:18

If anyone is in Christ, he is a new creation; old things have
passed away; behold, all things have become new.

2 CORINTHIANS 5:17

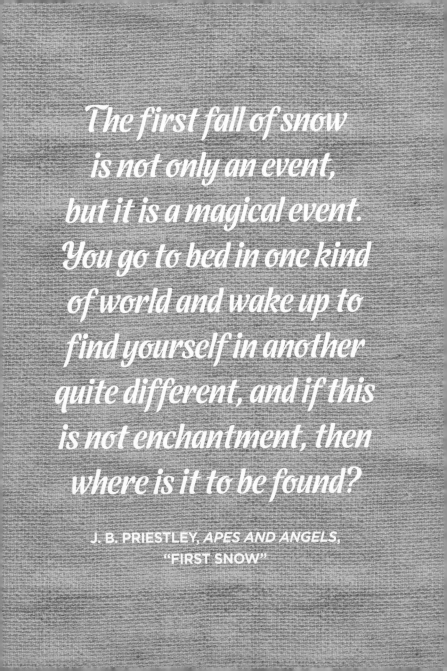

The first fall of snow
is not only an event,
but it is a magical event.
You go to bed in one kind
of world and wake up to
find yourself in another
quite different, and if this
is not enchantment, then
where is it to be found?

J. B. PRIESTLEY, *APES AND ANGELS*,
"FIRST SNOW"

Before the reward there must be labor. You plant before you harvest. You sow in tears before you reap in joy.

RALPH RANSOM,
STEPS ON THE STAIRWAY

Finishing the Work

The work of farming is never really done. Even in winter there is work to do—tending animals, cleaning tools, repairing machines. But many farmers like to talk about the moment the last of the crops are harvested. After a long season of planting and watering and gleaning, the job is done. The end of the harvest is a point of satisfaction, a threshold of one season leading to the next, when it can be said, "Well done." The Bible says that we are God's special handiwork. He is *constantly* cultivating us, growing us, and maturing us. Maybe you sense this in your life right now—that God has completed something in you and is starting another season of your life. What might that be?

Whenever someone turns to the Lord, the veil is taken away. For the Lord is the Spirit, and wherever the Spirit of the Lord is, there is freedom. So all of us who have had that veil removed can see and reflect the glory of the Lord. And the Lord—who is the Spirit—makes us more and more like him as we are changed into his glorious image.

2 CORINTHIANS 3:16-18, NLT

I thank my God upon every remembrance of you . . . being confident of this very thing, that He who has begun a good work in you will complete it until the day of Jesus Christ.

PHILIPPIANS 1:3, 6

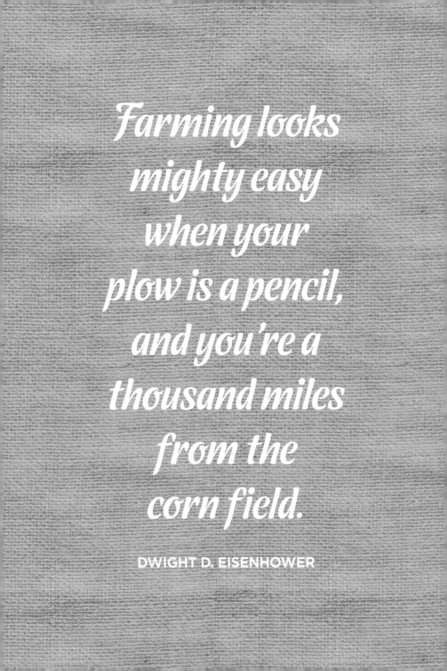

Farming looks
mighty easy
when your
plow is a pencil,
and you're a
thousand miles
from the
corn field.

DWIGHT D. EISENHOWER

Hard Work

City folk might never realize how much hard work is involved in farming. They might *think* they know, but until they spend a week in a farmer's muddy boots, they'll always underestimate the labor involved. Farmwork is also a way of life for the whole family. There's a country saying: "No one works harder than a farmer—except maybe a farmer's wife." Living the Christian life is hard work, too, and maybe it's harder than you thought. You seek every day to avoid sin and follow Jesus, but the temptations are strong and the circumstances difficult. Jesus never underestimates the labor involved; he says, "The gateway to life is very narrow and the road is difficult" (Matthew 7:14, NLT). But the alternative is even less attractive, and when you signed up for this gig, you inherited the promise of abundant spiritual life and eternal life in the age to come. "Is anything worth more than your soul?" (Mark 8:37, NLT). God's Kingdom is the "pearl of great value" (Matthew 13:46, NLT). God will strengthen you and help you make it to the harvest.

He said to them all, "If anyone desires to come after Me, let him deny himself, and take up his cross daily, and follow Me. For whoever desires to save his life will lose it, but whoever loses his life for My sake will save it."

LUKE 9:23-24

The Hope of Heaven

There are times when we have experiences that feel magical—when everything, just for a brief and fleeting moment, seems perfect. Perhaps the quiet wonder of a rural sunrise, a romantic evening with the one you love, or a joyous dinner with family when everyone is laughing offers a glimpse of what heaven might be like. The Amish have a saying: "Heaven's delights will far outweigh earth's difficulties." In the midst of your own challenges, consider pondering these experiences and memories of "heaven on earth." While God means for us to toil through the hard work of life, he gives us the hope of heaven to look forward to—an amazing and wonderful future. Keep your eyes fixed on Jesus and the promise of heaven-life with him.

We are citizens of heaven, where the Lord Jesus Christ lives. And we are eagerly waiting for him to return as our Savior. He will take our weak mortal bodies and change them into glorious bodies like his own, using the same power with which he will bring everything under his control.

PHILIPPIANS 3:20-21, NLT

*That was
such a happy
supper that
Laura wanted it
never to end.*

LAURA INGALLS WILDER,
THE LONG WINTER

The Joy of Country

The pleasure of country living is found in simply being there. You don't have to walk or drive to the show; it's all around you—in the morning dawn, the swaying fields of golden wheat, the dirt path lined with honeysuckle, leading down to the creek. Think of it all as God's joy, shared especially with you. That fading sun at twilight, spreading wide along the horizon, is his smile at the end of your day. Tarry with him there, and let his smile spark your joy as it reminds you of all he's done in your life. Rejoice and worship him as you enter into his pleasure.

God has made a home in the heavens for the sun. It bursts
forth like a radiant bridegroom after his wedding. It rejoices
like a great athlete eager to run the race. The sun rises at one
end of the heavens and follows its course to the other end.

PSALM 19:4-6, NLT

Those who live at the ends of the earth stand
in awe of your wonders. From where the sun rises
to where it sets, you inspire shouts of joy.

PSALM 65:8, NLT

Notes

page 12   **The one thing that is worse:** Suzanne Woods Fisher, *Amish Proverbs: Words of Wisdom from the Simple Life*, expanded ed. (Grand Rapids, MI: Revell, 2012), 85.

page 32   **What other people think of you:** Fisher, *Amish Proverbs*, 75.

page 34   **In one episode of** Little House on the Prairie: See *Little House on the Prairie*, season 2, episode 9, "Ebenezer Sprague," dailymotion.com /video/x6def9n.

page 34   **"Learn from your failures":** Fisher, *Amish Proverbs*, 95.

page 36   **If you wish to be happy:** Fisher, *Amish Proverbs*, 25.

page 43   **Every miracle Jesus does:** Fisher, *Amish Proverbs*, 48.

page 44   **God's blessing gained:** Edwin Miller Fogel, *Proverbs of the Pennsylvania Germans* (Lancaster, PA: Lancaster Press, 2010), 192.

page 61   **"Authenticity is the daily practice":** Brené Brown, *The Gifts of Imperfection* (New York: Random House, 2010), 68.

page 70   **"Brokenness is nothing to be ashamed of":** Elisa Morgan, "The Beauty of Broken," *God Hears Her* podcast, episode 2, 31:53, https:// www.godhearsher.org/podcast/episode-02-beauty-of-broken.

page 73   **Scientists have proven that gardening:** See Robyn Francis, "Why Gardening Makes You Happy and Cures Depression," Permaculture College Australia—Djanbung Gardens, accessed July 1, 2021, https:// permaculture.com.au/why-gardening-makes-you-happy-and-cures -depression/.

page 74   ***"Gardening by the moon"***: See Jamie McLeod, "Why Do We Garden
by the Moon?" *Farmers' Almanac*, updated July 16, 2021, https://
www.farmersalmanac.com/why-garden-by-the-moon
-20824?nowprocket=1.

page 90   ***When you speak, always remember***: Fisher, *Amish Proverbs*, 69.

page 92   ***In order to mold his people***: Fisher, *Amish Proverbs*, 99.

page 110   ***"Lord of the Dance"***: "Lord of the Dance," words by Sydney Carter,
copyright © 1963, Stainer & Bell Ltd, London, England (admin
Hope Publishing Company, Carol Stream, IL 60188). All rights
reserved.

page 130   ***A Psychology Today *article talks about***: See Seth Gillihan,
"10 Mental Health Benefits of Gardening," *Psychology Today*, June 19,
2019, https://www.psychologytoday.com/us/blog/think-act-be
/201906/10-mental-health-benefits-gardening.

page 154   ***"Our country would be better served"***: Bob Dotson, *American Story:
A Lifetime Search for Ordinary People Doing Extraordinary Things*
(New York: Plume, 2014), 36.

page 182   ***"Heaven's delights will far outweigh"***: Fisher, *Amish Proverbs*, 99.